Published in 2022 by Orange Mosquito
An Imprint of Welbeck Children's Limited
part of Welbeck Publishing Group.

Based in London and Sydney.

www.welbeckpublishing.com

Design and layout © Mosquito Books Barcelona, SL 2021
Text © Soledad Romero Mariño 2021
Illustration © Montse Galbany 2021
Translated by Howard Curtis
Publisher: Margaux Durigon
Production: Clare Hennessy

ISBN: 9871914519208
eISBN: 9781914519215

Printed in China

10 9 8 7 6 5 4 3 2 1

FSC
www.fsc.org
MIX
Paper from
responsible sources
FSC® C020056

## Disclaimer:

Awesome Accidents is intended for general informational purposes only and should not be relied upon as exact timeline of events or promoting or encouraging any activity that maybe dangerous or injurious to the user of this book. All readers under the legal age within their jurisdiction should seek advice and consent from their parent(s) or guardian(s) before relying on any information detailed in this book.

The publisher and the author make no representations or warranties of any kind, express or implied, with respect to the accuracy, completeness, merchantability, fitness, suitability or currency of the contents of this book, and specifically disclaim to the extent permitted by law.

No animals were harmed in the making of this book, but a few were bribed into helping out.

# AWESOME ACCIDENTS
## 19 DISCOVERIES THAT CHANGED THE WORLD

ORANGE
M·O·S·Q·U·I·T·O

**Soledad Romero Mariño · Montse Galbany**

# Introduction

Accidents are an essential step in every learning curve, every piece of research, every act of creation. Through trial and error, we often find the right solution and the human race evolves.

**There is no need to be afraid of making mistakes. Error is the great teacher and is always ready to show us the way to success.**

Sometimes, a mistake or an accident ends up saving millions of lives, like the discovery of penicillin. At other times, a false step leads to an unexpected creation that make our lives easier and happier, like safety matches or even the delicious French desert Tarte Tatin.

AWESOME ACCIDENTS is a tribute to human trial and error. It is an illustrated history of the crazy mistakes that gave us wonderful discoveries. Don't be afraid of getting things wrong; mistakes guide us and show us the way to success.

# Coffee

## Ethiopia, 600

Kaldi, an
Ethiopian
goatherd

Walking his flock on the high
slopes of Kaffa, the goatherd
Kaldi happened to notice
how energetic his goats
became after they ate a
particular red fruit sprouting
on some small wild bushes.

Kaldi, attracted by the stimulating effects it had on his goats, gathered the fruit and handed it over to the imam of the mosque in the village where he lived. The imam analyzed the goatherd's discovery and made a concoction from it. But the taste was too strong and bitter; disgusted, he threw the fruit into the fire.

An awesome accident! The toasted aroma smelled wonderful.

The first cup of coffee was made from seeds rescued from a fire in a small mosque in Ethiopia. It turned out to be a delicious drink as well as an effective remedy against sleepiness, and it gradually won over the entire world.

# Fireworks

## China, 820

There are many ideas about how fireworks were invented. One involves a cook ... In the kitchens of old China, it was common to use a mixture of salt, sulfur, and coal for preserving food. But on one occasion, a cook accidentally put the mixture too close to the fire and it blew up!

An anonymous cook

### An awesome accident!
### A fizz of light, color and fire
### lit up the kitchen.

The cook was amazed by the magical effect of his explosion. Without knowing it, he had created fireworks.

At first, fireworks were used in small religious ceremonies. It was believed that the explosions had the power to chase away ghosts and evil spirits. But later, during the Song dynasty (960-1279), their use changed and people started to fill the skies with light and color during great festivals.

Over the centuries, master craftsmen learned to control the delicate combustion and added different colors, offering fantastic spectacles considered to be works of art.

# Champagne

## France, 1670

In the year 1668, the monk Pierre Pérignon was transferred to the Abbey of Hautvillers.

Avoiding bubbles in the wine ...

Champagne
Dom. Perignon

The Abbey was in ruins, but it was situated amid the fabulous vineyards of the French region of Champagne. Pérignon was determined to save the Abbey by creating the most delicious wine in the world. He had the best grapes (the fruit that wine is made from) in France, and he also had an exceptional palate. It was said that, being blind, Pérignon had developed an amazing sense of taste and he could even tell which vineyard the grape he was eating came from. All year Pérignon worked hard, but when the heat of spring arrived, he had to face a new challenge.

# An awesome accident!

When Pierre Pérignon drank his work and experienced the taste and fizz on his palate.

## Millions of small, sparkling bubbles appeared in the wine – the corks shot out and the bottles exploded.

Pérignon tried many things to avoid the uncontrollable bubbles, but without success. It was only when he resigned to throw a whole year's work out that he decided to try his unsuccessful creation.

An awesome accident! When Pierre Pérignon tasted his work and experienced the flavor and fizz on his palate, he cried for joy: "Come quickly! I'm drinking the stars!" He had managed to create champagne, one of the most popular wines in the world.

From then on, Pérignon bottled the liquid in English glass and fastened the corks with wires to stop them firing off. He made an opportunity out of a crisis and champagne began to appear on the most exclusive tables as a symbol of celebration and joy.
Cheers!

Pierre Pérignon, Benedictine monk

# The Eraser

## UK, 1770

Edward Nairne devoted his whole life to inventing complex electrical machines, optical instruments, and barometers. He was an applied engineer (meaning he used math and science to design useful things) who gained a considerable international reputation.

One day, as he was sketching a design for a new machine, Nairne made a mistake. He reached for the ball of breadcrumbs he usually used to erase pencil marks, and mistakenly picked up a piece of rubber.

**Edward Nairne**

Barometer

a
b
c
d

Telescope

a
b
c
d

**Ball of breadcrumbs**

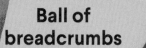

Awesome accident!

Piece of rubber

An awesome accident!
Nairne easily erased the pencil
marks with the piece of rubber.
The astute inventor soon realized
that he had created the eraser.
It was his simplest invention but
also the one that has been most
widely used ever since he
created it.

# The Battery

## Italy, 1800

**Luigi Galvani**

**Alessandro Volta**

Alessandro Volta's parents wanted their son to be a lawyer, but he had other plans. Drawn to natural phenomena, Volta began doing scientific experiments on his own. At the same time, his friend and fellow scientist Luigi Galvani was also conducting experiments in his laboratory. In one of these experiments, Galvani was dissecting a dead frog fixed to a brass hook. He touched its leg with an iron scalpel and accidentally caused the leg to move.

## Awesome accident!

Galvani had discovered that the contact between two metals and the muscles of a frog generated an electric current. He called it "animal electricity," convinced that it was the frog's tissue that generated the electricity.

But Volta, thanks to his colleague's discovery, reached a different, revolutionary conclusion. After several more experiments, Volta confirmed that it was not the animal's tissue that generated the current, but the contact of two metals with certain chemical compounds.

On the basis of these conclusions, Volta designed a battery, called a "pile": being a number of silver and zinc discs piled alternately, separated by pieces of cloth soaked in salt water.

## The circuit between the components generated electricity!

His creation was a resounding success. The whole scientific community recognised his merit and Volta went down in history for having turned a laboratory accident into a great invention for humanity.

→ Copper
→ Brine
→ Zinc

He touched its leg with the iron scalpel and accidentally caused the leg to move.

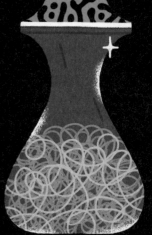

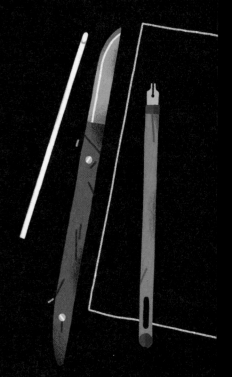

Fig: 1.

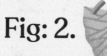

Fig: 2.

# The safety match

## UK, 1826

John Walker was an English chemist and pharmacist. In the back room of his pharmacy, he often spent hours doing experiments.

One fine day, trying to create a new explosive, Walker mixed together the chemicals antimony sulfate and potassium chlorate with rubber, starch, and sugar. Walker was conscientiously stirring the mixture with a wooden stick when he noticed that a solid residue had formed on the end of the stick.

sugar

rubber

starch

potassium chlorate

antimony sulphate

**John Walker**

When Walker tried to clean the stick, by rubbing it against the floor, it accidentally caught fire.

Awesome accident!

He had just invented the safety match.

Walker called his invention "friction matches" and began to sell them in his pharmacy. But unfortunately, he did not patent the invention and it was Samuel Jones who, seeing the potential of the product, improved and patented it. Jones marketed the matches under the name "lucifers," which means **"bearers of light".**

S.JONES'S
LUCIFERS
MADE IN
ENGLAND

The match was the result of chance, but it was one of the greatest inventions in history.

It allowed human beings to obtain fire instantaneously!

# Potato chips

## USA, 1853

George Crum was a chef at a prestigious New York restaurant called Moon's Lake House.

On August 24, 1853, Cornelius Vanderbilt (a multi-millionaire businessman) came into the restaurant. This event would change the chef's life forever.

George Crum

Vanderbilt asked for a dish of fried potatoes. Crum carefully made the best dish of fried potatoes he could. But the great magnate sent it back: the potatoes were too thick and underdone..

The chef, being a patient man, made the dish again, cutting the potatoes very thin and frying them for longer. But Vanderbilt again sent the dish back: the potatoes were still too thick and raw. Crum's patience ran out. He took his revenge by cutting the potatoes as thin as paper and frying them for so long that it was impossible to pierce them with a fork without breaking them. In addition, Crum covered them with a lot of salt. He was sure his dish was a huge, inedible mess.

## Awesome accident!

Vanderbilt went crazy for it. He declared that he had never eaten such delicious potatoes and this attempted failure of a dish went on to become the most popular snack in the world.

This unsuccessful dish went on to become the most popular snack in the world.

# Artificial dye

## UK, 1856

By the middle of the 19th century, British troops were stationed in half of the world and thousands of them were dying of malaria.

**Quinine**

**Malaria mosquito**

At that time, the only remedy for the disease was quinine. However, quinine was a scarce, expensive substance derived from a tropical tree in South America. So British laboratories were hard at work trying to produce it artificially. Among those devoting themselves to this work were the famous German chemist August Wilhelm von Hofmann and his young pupil William Henry Perkin. They thought they could synthesize quinine by oxidizing another, more common and cheaper substance. So it was that Perkin, while his master was away, tried out the idea in his small home laboratory. Perkin's experiment was a failure; he only managed to produce a dark tar. But when trying to clean the result of his mistake with alcohol, he discovered that the tar was actually a wonderful, indelible purple substance.

## Awesome accident!

Perkin had just created the first synthetic dye. Since ancient times, the spectacular color purple had been coveted because it was the most difficult to obtain naturally. And so, this unexpected discovery turned out to be an incredible success.

Perkin & Sons

PURPLE
Perkin & Sons

At the age of only 18, Perkin patented the idea and together with his father and brother started a factory to make dyes. By the time he was 21 he was a millionaire, and at 36 he retired from the business to devote himself to research and give back to chemistry all it had given him.

# X-rays

## Germany, 1895

**Cathode ray tube**

**Wilhelm Röntgen**

The physicist Wilhelm Röntgen did not like attending long lectures or scientific conferences. As a matter of fact, his publications were not well received by his colleagues, who found them uncreative. But things would change forever on November 8, 1895. In his laboratory late at night, Röntgen was observing the violet fluorescence emitted by cathode light rays*. It was at this point that, thanks to the total darkness in which he was working, he happened to notice a dim yellowish-green gleam given off by a screen covered in a layer of barium platinocyanide which he had in the laboratory.

---

* A phenomenon linked to electricity recently discovered and highly studied by the physicists at the end of 19th century.

Awesome accident! Röntgen realized that the mysterious light emitted by the rays were capable of penetrating opaque material. He called the light "X-rays." Röntgen shut himself in his laboratory and performed all kinds of experiments to make the most of his discovery. Being fond of photography, Röntgen thought of using photosensitive plates to record the effect of the rays as they went through different objects. He must have had quite a fright when he photographed his wife's hand—he could see her bones!

Screen covered in barium platinocyanide

He must have had quite a fright when he photographed his wife's hand. He could see her bones!

This discovery would revolutionize medicine forever. X-rays were capable of going through skin, meaning doctors could see inside the human body!

When the results of his research were published, they created a great stir in the scientific community. In 1901, Röntgen was awarded the Nobel Prize in Physics for his accidental discovery.

# Radioactivity

France, 1896

After discovering the existence of X-rays, Wilhelm Röntgen shared his studies with his colleagues.

A French physicist named Henri Becquerel was particularly interested in these studies and, inspired by the achievement of his German colleague, set out to study the phosphorescence (a type of light) emitted by uranium (a metal).

Becquerel was able to confirm that the phosphorescence of uranium went through black paper and could expose photographic plates. The radiation (a type of energy) from it was really powerful and so Becquerel was sure that it came from the sun.

Becquerel always made sure that the uranium sat out, to receive a good dose of sun. But then came days of rain and Becquerel put the metal substance away with the photographic plates in a drawer.

Awesome accident! When Becquerel went back to the uranium, he found that it had exposed the photographic plate. The only possible explanation was that the radiation came from the metal itself. Becquerel had just discovered what Marie Curie would later call radioactivity.

In 1903, Marie Curie and her husband Pierre Curie received the Nobel Prize in Physics together with Becquerel for the discovery of r adioactivity.

The radiation from the metal was really powerful and Becquerel was sure that it came from the sun.

# Tarte Tatin

France, 1900

Stéphanie and Caroline Tatin

During the delightful, prosperous Belle Époque (1870-1914), the sisters Stéphanie and Caroline Tatin inherited from their father a charming hotel in the little town of Lamotte-Beuvron, south of Orléans (France). The place had become a center for hunting, much frequented by the middle classes arriving from Paris by train. Caroline, the younger sister, was in charge of receiving guests while Stéphanie, the older sister, was responsible for the kitchen. The two of them created a friendly and welcoming atmosphere.

One day, Stéphanie became distracted and overbaked some apples. In order not to waste the slightly burnt dish, she improvised and covered it with dough.

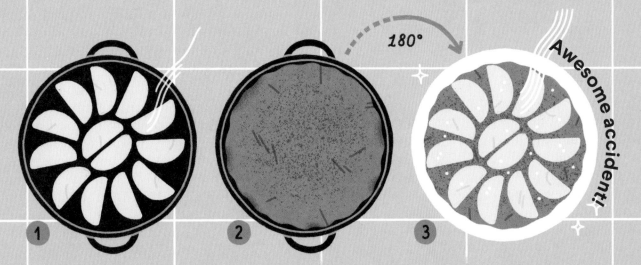

**1**  **2**  **3**

180°

Awesome accident!

**Awesome accident!** When she took the accidental dish from the oven and turned it over to serve it, Stéphanie found she had created a delicious upside-down, caramelized apple cake. The innovative dessert was a great success with guests and soon became its star attraction.

It is said that a guest of the hotel—a famous pastry chef—copied it in a restaurant in Paris, where it became a resounding success in high society. The pastry chef, showing great professional integrity, gave the cake the name of its creator. From that point, Tarte Tatin began its unstoppable journey around the world, winning over the most discerning palates.

# Plastic

Belgium, 1907

Leo Hendrik Baekeland was born to a poor family. His father was a cobbler and his mother a domestic servant. Against her husband's wishes, she saw to it that her son studied chemistry, mechanics, and photography.

In 1889, the young man was granted a scholarship to study at the University of New York. It was there that Baekeland produced his first great invention: a revolutionary photographic paper, which meant that photographs could be developed quickly and cheaply. The Kodak company bought his patent for a fortune.

Baekeland was now extremely rich, but he did not give up his passion for research and he set up a laboratory in his own home.

At that time, the booming electrical industry needed insulating material for cables. The only material available was a natural resin made by insects and it was very hard to come by. Researchers were working on the creation of a synthetic resin to replace the natural one. The first experiments were crushing failures; it was impossible to control the processes of synthesis and scientists only managed to produce a tar-like substance which destroyed laboratory equipment.

**The original 'Bakelizer' for checking pressure and temperature.**

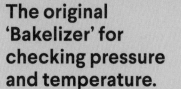

Leo Hendrik Baekeland

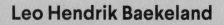

**Bakelite was the first ever plastic, created with a failed material, thanks to the determination of a great scientist who <u>never gave up</u>.**

# Penicillin

## UK, 1928

Alexander Fleming

During the First World War, the doctor Alexander Fleming attended soldiers wounded in battle. Shocked by the great suffering and high mortality rate of those with infected machine-gun wounds, he returned to London determined to find a cure.

In the laboratory in the basement of Saint Mary's Hospital, the doctor began his experiments. Fleming cultivated bacteria in search of a substance that would destroy them, but after a number of failed attempts, he decided to take a holiday. For a month, he left his experiments out in the hospital's untidy laboratory.

When Fleming returned to work, he found his research ruined. He had left the samples near an open window and mold had contaminated the cultures of bacteria.

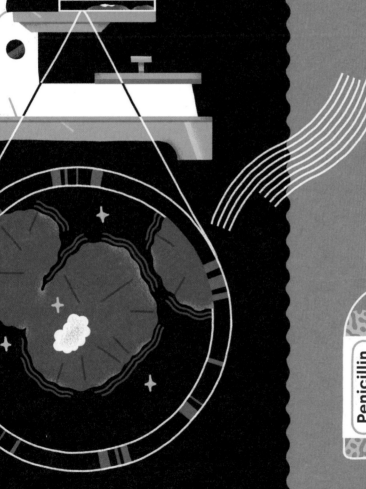

**Awesome accident!** When Fleming examined the disaster through a microscope, he discovered that the bacteria had been killed by the mold— specifically the Penicillium fungus. Alexander Fleming had created the first antibiotic, his cure for infections.

Penicillin was able to save millions of lives, which is why it is considered one of the most important discoveries in history. In 1945, Fleming shared the Nobel Prize in medicine with his colleagues Ernst Boris Chain and Howard Walter Florey.

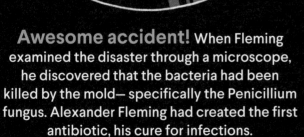

# The Big Bang theory

USA, 1930

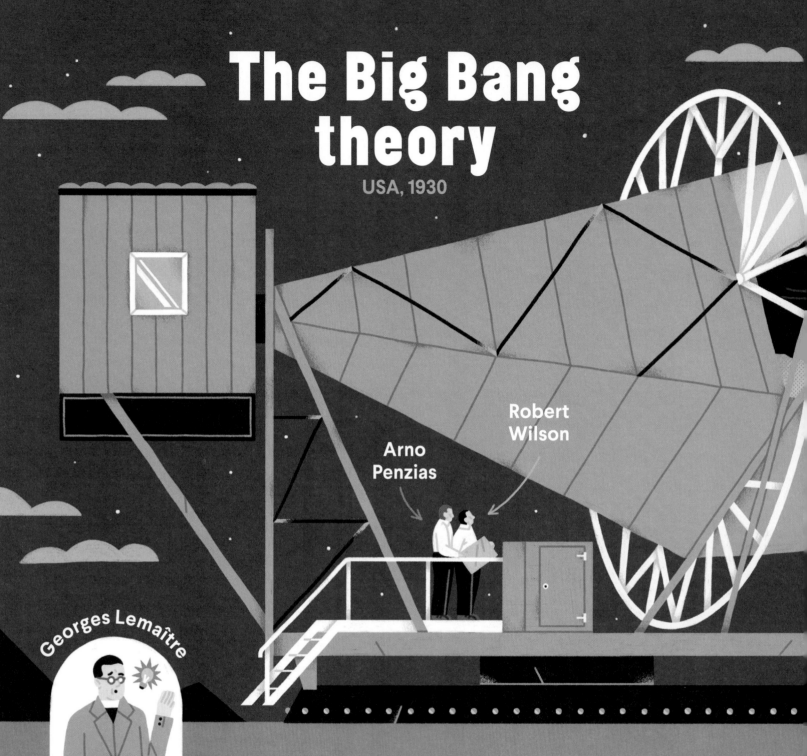

Robert Wilson

Arno Penzias

Georges Lemaître

In 1927, the priest Georges Lemaître suggested that the origin of the universe had been a huge explosion. It was only later that this theory began to be known as the Big Bang.

Great scientists supported it, even asserting that this explosion had given rise to radiation (a type of energy) that was still traveling through the universe. This radiation was dubbed CMB (Cosmic Microwave Background), but it was an unconfirmed theory.

Several decades later, in New Jersey, the physicists Arno Penzias and Robert Wilson were working on a new kind of antenna and something went wrong.

They tuned into a strange noise coming from space. They could not silence this mysterious interference in any way and

**Awesome accident!** The physicists had built an antenna capable of tuning in to the sound of the radiation created in the great explosion.

Robert Henry Dicke

they thought the antenna was a total disaster.

**Awesome accident!** The physicists had actually built an antenna capable of tuning in to the sound of the radiation (CMB) created in the great explosion. This discovery fully confirmed the Big Bang theory!

In 1978 Arno Penzias and Robert Wilson were awarded the Nobel Prize. But in all fairness, we should acknowledge the part played by the physicist Robert Henry Dicke – he was the one who worked out where the mysterious noise was coming from, but all he got was a pat on the back from his colleagues. *C'est La Vie* (that's life).

# Super glue

## USA, 1940

Dr. Harry
Coover

During the Second World War, the development of new technologies was one of the most effective strategies for defeating the enemy. A chemist named Dr. Harry Coover was one of those recruited for this task by the United States Army.

In his laboratory, Coover experimented with acrylates (a chemical) in the hope of creating clear plastic telescopic lenses. By mistake, Coover created an extremely sticky substance that stuck to everything it touched and ruined his laboratory equipment.

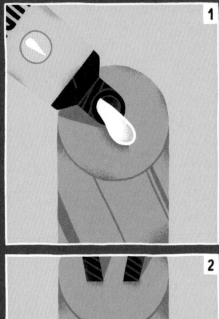

New Super Glue Try it!

## Awesome accident!

Coover had invented Super Glue – the strongest glue in the world. But it wasn't until 9 years later, after the war, that Coover and his team rescued the substance and recognized it as a revolutionary invention.

In 1958, the company where Coover worked marketed it. Super Glue was now on sale!

SUPER GLUE

KODAK

CYANOACRYLATE

# Velcro

## Switzerland, 1941

Electrician engineer
**Georges de Mestral**

George de Mestral was always inquisitive and creative. He was only 12 when he built a toy plane which he later patented. De Mestral then studied engineering in one of the best schools of science and technology, after which he began working in a commercial company.

In his free time, de Mestral liked walking his dog in the Alpine meadows. But when he returned home, he would have to remove tiny, annoying prickly burrs from his clothes and his dog's hair.

## Awesome accident!

These nasty burrs were the inspiration de Mestral needed to create a new, effective, and rapid system for binding two pieces of material—one side had hooks and the other had loops.

De Mestral called his invention Velcro, and although at first he found it hard to effectively copy what nature had created, he finally succeeded.

Initially, clothes manufacturers did not buy into the idea of Velcro—it was too innovative. But then NASA bought de Mestral's Velcro tapes to hold together objects as they floated in space. Suddenly, de Mestral's invention went from being an oddity to being a space age revolution. From the 1960s onward, Velcro became a big success in the fashion industry.

**Velcro was a big success in the fashion industry.**

# The Microwave oven

**USA, 1945**

Percy Spencer did not have an easy life. He lost his parents when he was a child and had to leave school to start working in a paper mill. When he was old enough, he joined the United States Navy and finally received a technical education.

When he left the navy, Spencer started working for Raytheon, a company specializing in the manufacture of military components. Spencer's contribution was outstanding. He suggested improvements in the process that helped to increase production from 17 to 2600 magnetrons* a day.

One fine day, while Spencer was working in front of a magnetron, he discovered that a chocolate bar he had in his pocket had melted.

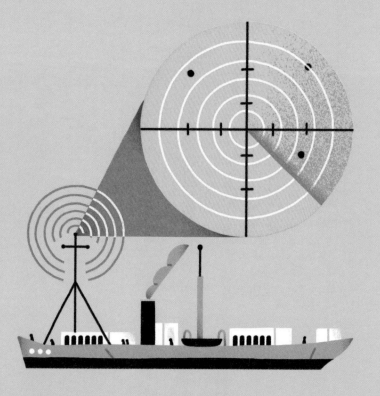

\* Magnetrons are the main components of radar systems. Their function is to transform electrical energy into electromagnetic microwaves which the radar system uses to measure distances and speeds, among other things.

**The kernels started to sputter around the laboratory!**

Engineer
Percy Spencer

**Awesome accident!** This unfortunate – and sticky – accident made him realize that electromagnetic microwaves generated heat and could be used to cook food. Excited, he put a bowl of popcorn in front of the magnetron. The kernels started to sputter around the laboratory!

Spencer immediately began work on designing the microwave oven. Just a few years later, the microwave oven went on the market and soon became all the rage in modern kitchens.

# Post-its

## USA, 1970

Spencer Silver had only recently completed his studies when he started working for 3M—an American conglomerate known for innovating new products and technologies. The young chemist arrived at the vast corporation with the ambition of conquering the world. With this motivation, Silver shut himself up in the laboratories, trying to create a high-strength adhesive to be used in building planes. But the young man failed miserably—his glue only managed to stick two sheets of paper together. What was worse, it was so weak that the two sheets of paper came unstuck easily.

**Awesome accident!** Silver had created a super-special adhesive. Although at first nobody knew what to do with it, years later, his colleague Arthur Fry found the perfect use for it.

Pads of sheets coated with this adhesive were produced. Each sheet could easily be detached from the pad and could be stuck again as a marker or reminder on almost anything: folders, books, filing cabinets, computers, window panes, tables, and so on.

Spencer Silver

Arthur Fry

Good idea

Important note!

!!!!

3M

**The corporation's office assistants were the first to use them.**

Almost instinctively, they used up hundreds of sheets writing notes and sticking them all over the place. These pads were eventually called Post-its and were one of 3M's biggest successes.

At last, Spencer Silver, thanks to his failed adhesive, achieved a sought-after success.

# Mapping the Ocean Currents

Aleutian Islands

Hong Kong

This story begins with a storm in the middle of the Pacific Ocean. The waves reached a height of 26 feet and fierce winds lashed the Chinese freighter from Hong Kong that was trying to reach the coast of Washington.

But in the icy waters of Alaska, twelve containers fell overboard and were lost on the ocean bed, like so many others on so many occasions. But this time, one of the containers opened and in the middle of the furious storm 28,000 yellow rubber ducks fell into the ocean. It was a genuine natural disaster.

Washington

**Curtis
Ebbesmeyer**

**Awesome accident!** After the
initial lamentations, a team of scientists
realised that these drifting ducks could play
an important role in a study of the marine
currents that link the Pacific and the North
Atlantic.

From that day on, the scientists devoted
themselves to following the yellow ducks on
the high seas, all the way to the distant coasts
of Scotland.

Finally, the oceanographer Curtis
Ebbesmeyer managed to reconstruct the
ducks' trajectory and established that an
object takes three years to complete a circle
of the oceans in these currents. Thanks to his
study, he also obtained valuable information
on the effects of global warming on ocean
currents.

The wandering ducks ended up with a large
fan club of collectors all over the world.

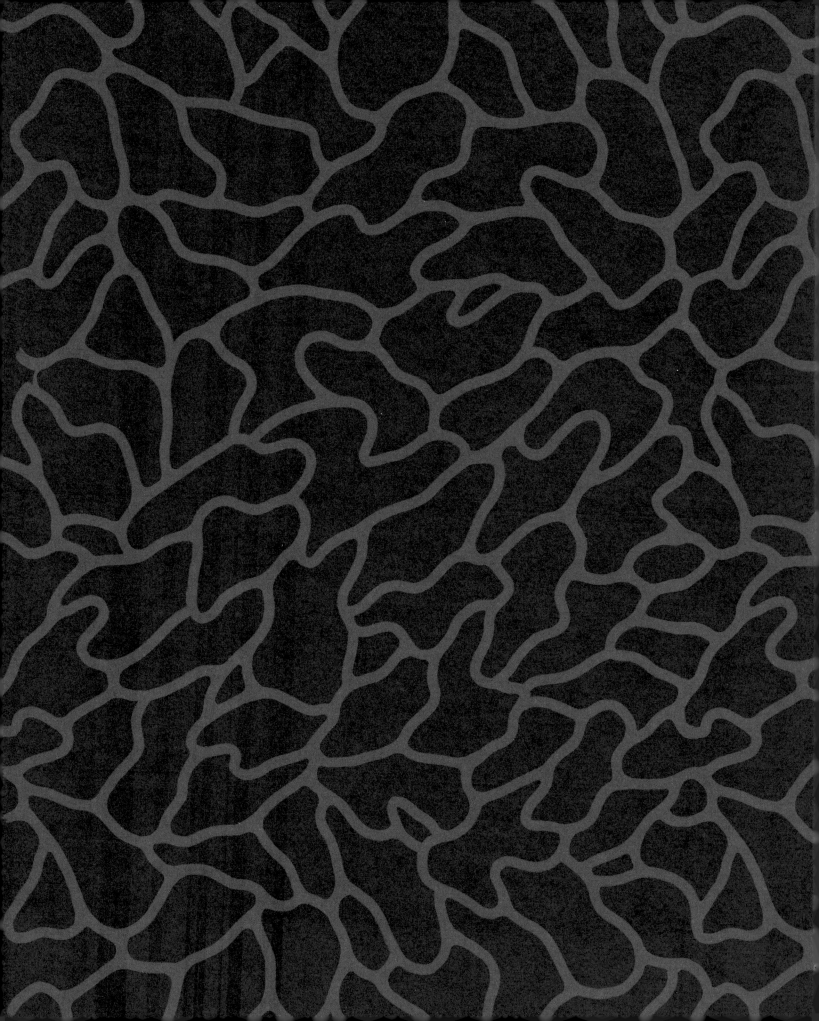